The Wasp in the Jar

A Poetry Collection
By
Kerri Anne Byrnes

God bless you,

Kerri Anne Byrnes

ISBN 978-1-329-76223-7

Dedication

This book is dedicated to all of the people who have made the last year unbearably difficult. Thank you for providing me with enough material to ensure that I will be engaging in a multitude of character-building exercises for the next millennia.

Polly-Girl-Gone

Polly-Girl-Gone

Running through a field in flower

Monochrome of iridescent blue

It's waving

Stripped off her gingham dress and put on a Batman suit

Imagination running wilder than sea-salt-wind

That lashes at the break of shoreline

Polly-Girl-Gone

Dancing on, spinning with a twelve-foot python in her hands

Lightning arcs through a night-dark mane

And laughter crackles like crystal streams

Polly-Girl-Gone

Electric jubilance guiding careless steps

Her candy smile – sweet yet somehow cunning –

Appears and disappears in firefly winks

I go with Polly-Girl now

To the summer-soft field

To the place where my innocence dreams it's still breathing

The Throwaway Palette

The colors used to tell the story were bright

Straight out of the box

Sticky and sharp

They tasted like moonlit rain in an acid downpour

A stain running down

Running on

She fanned the picture of the life her fantasies knew so well

Blew gently on incongruent bubbles

They popped, incompatible with the rosy-shaded world she'd formed

Set up for the fantastic – but –

So fantastic a fall

Landing face-down on the canvas, she drowned in blood-warm paint

The Stamp

The antichrist was born with a 666

Supposedly – he came in with Lucifer's

Stamp of Approval

Didn't have to boil people alive or

Flash through the night in black-dog form – He just Was

I was born with a need to be admired

By family, by friends, even by foe

Fighting for a moment at a time

When I could be ten feet taller

And more talented than an aerialist

And I already am so good at jumping through high hoops with no net

Other people's

They took my thunder, ripping it out of my baby-lion mouth

Whenever there was a shine on me

Coward-me hid in the dark

Chewing fingernails and squawking

All I was good for was warming an egg

I stood up

And fell down

As they tore apart my clumsy evening gown

That they told me never fit me

And now – I wake up in the morning

Naked, I scrutinize with mirrors

Looking for my own Stamp

So I can be FDA-approved

Certified as useful meat

North of Hell, South of Heaven

They ask me how are you
They can't even imagine
What I trudge through
I just smile as I say
North of Hell, south of Heaven
The devil's on your coat-tails, you tell me
And I proudly show the broken halo
I stole from St. Peter at the Gates
But I'm still not far from a giggle
And I clap you on the back in hearty spell
Should have lied and said I'm doing swell
But fifties' colloquialisms don't quite fit this eighties' kid
I never used to bullshit the masses
Would unfurl my honesty like a barbed cloak
Now I'm likely to swallow back nails and hug you
Though you inspire me to retch

Unbroken Novenas

Unbroken Novenas

Prayers to the Saintly Ones

Whose refuge with God is immutable

Rosary dangles like candy on rope

She's begging again Lord

For a sensible route

For a moment of freedom and a chance to start new

A new Church to replace the broken Behemoth

For the lascivious teams to stop trading priest-players

Her voice cracking alleluia

She drowns in the voice of her plea to be found

Haunted

Hunting for God in the spire

Rip the Band-Aid Off

Gaping wound, bleeding slow

Ratty rubber strings still sticking in – God it hurts!

I wanted the truth, wanted it now

So my eyes plastered themselves greedily

To an LCD-screen, roving over the sticky juice of poison-fruit – Such words!

I didn't go blind, vision's microscope sharp!

The so-called wisdom in articles punctuated by iPad-ads

Differs from the words in dusty library tomes?

The lies that paint the matrix shapes

Coat your skin with scented lotions from XYZ celebrity –

A steal at $9.99 or whatever a soul goes for these days –

Cheap when everyone's selling

I grew up, cgi-techno-girl in a virtual world

I grew up when I finally caved in

To the Powers-That-Be and returned their haughty grin

If only I had opened my sad eyes on the day I was born

Glistening meat sandwiched between the teeth of wars

Another pawn in a disturbing world-wide match run by

Evil Queens and Kings – yet their finery bespoke innocence!

It would have been better

To adjust slowly to their Rule

But I fell in the hole with Thumper and the other rabbits

And screamed while they cuddled with their horned lap-demons

Who played with my tangled hair and whispered, "Rip the Band-Aid off"

The Impotent Adept

They told me in a not-too-distant past

About the power I possess –

Power that is locked in someone else's Keepsake Box

Is it with the treasure someone stole

From the last year of my Normal Life?

Is this magic somehow confined to someone else's cauldron?

When, when I seek the omnipotent deity

He or she keeps no check for me

Only checks and balances

I wanted to be harmless

I wanted charm yet was charmless

My robes are simple Wal-Mart cloth

Falling off at the shoulder

That's a stain, not a clip of precious metal

And that's a puddle of my self-esteem on the floor

Not the water for Ritual

Where are my successes?

Where are the black-cat familiars I seek?

Magic is nothing when it doesn't work

And spells are incoherent ramblings when

The actor onstage is an impotent Adept

World-Class Ass

He's a world-class ass

Casanova to extremes

Dingle-dangling his ding-a-ling

Ah, chalk it up to practice!

Wasting wives and mistresses like paper

At a preschool

World-class ass

Conspicuous consumption

And condom-sheathed commodity

He's pleased to be!

Leaving behind a conflagration

Which eats away his careful life

He skates away, omnipotent, and revels in his charm

Writing

Sometimes I write when I'm writhing

I blow my energetic load

Two feet from a hospital

It's ceaseless noise

And bugged-out eyes

While the doctor deadpans

She's not fighting for it

Or fighting for me

Sometimes I write

When she's arriving

In the soul-home loaded

With strawberry shortcake

Which no appetite can reach

The Heart in Me (Adulterer's Cry)

The heart in me says Now and cannot be withheld

From the blooming flower

The Grecian beauty

I dream of lips strong on mine

As my patient wife sleeps, curling into me

A voice I try to quiet stirs my fantasies

They both have dark hair

But eyes that tell different tales

Tales I cannot bear to hear

Especially the haunting ones of loss of my love

The heart of me

Turns in on itself

Hating itself for beating too fast

Too hard for all the wrong reasons

But for all the right feelings

For the woman who still makes me doubt all I have

America

America, the once-proud nation of self-starters and innovators

Sinks into the mire of obsolescence

American Dreamers turned Silent Slaves

The green poison dye of fiat currency

Snakes through veins, bleeding into jaundice

The feudal lords of the Federal Reserve

Laughing and lying as they stroke each other's backs

Can we come back and rebuild our homeland?

I see hope on the horizon

As the horseman of the apocalypse still carry silver and gold

In their yellowing teeth

Galloping for the love of this nation and her people

Am I, and I smile as I make the perfect trade

Illusion for Security, Worthless green rectangles for Honesty

Pistachio Ice Cream

Eyes so brown and bright

Shone like tumbled stones as I held your weakened hand

You were still in there

Flowing through the grim-grey pallor

And you still made jokes

Though they were thinner than paper

The pink plush of a stuffed animal

Swam in your bedsheets

You moved to reach for water and my heart broke

As you shook and water dribbled down your chin

The undignified sucking sound

Of a tube that's part of you now – will be – was

The blood and fluids moving in and out

Of stained clear tubes with dirty-seeming tape

They talked in baby-voice to a grown woman

And reminded you that

Pistachio ice cream is your favorite

And to try not to let it melt

I still hold your hand, feel you grip me

For dear life as your life fades

They Always Come

They always come

Those poor souls who crossed the final road

Sometimes confused

As after a tragedy in which they had the starring role

No Oscars forthcoming for *that* performance!

Sometimes sad

Because people they held onto can hold them no more

Sometimes angry

Vengeance guiding their hands to further damage

And sometimes joyful

Peacefully floating and lightly laughing

Eager to ease the pain of the ones picked last for the team

Whether or not they left on purpose

Or for a purpose

Or purposefully fought for their life and lost

They always come

And I always lead them Home

Numbers

From childhood worth was measured in Numbers

Numbers of My Little Ponies in the red closet toy box

Dollars in your allowance or from First Communion gifts

How many children could come to the pool party in June

And grades on all your tests at school

20/80 when you got that first pair of eyeglasses at Collin Creek Mall

By middle school numbers of valentines you didn't receive

In high school it was GPA and times you hit the honor roll

In college it was sex partners

And if that was 0.0 your reputation was worse than if it was infinity

Adult life's numbers are so much more

Confusing

Illusory and useless

Credit score says you're responsible or impulsive

Statistics at work say nothing of how reliable you are

How you come early to work

Or understand the complexity of a software program

Number of "friends" on social media sites

That's 1,000 people you can't call if your Corolla breaks down on I-95

Or worse, in the desert between Palm Springs and Barstow

Or 2,000 followers on Twitter who neither listen to or heed your advice

Yet surround you like a prophet or cult-leader

Numbers aren't real anymore

A cognizant self-aware spiritual being should know that

Doesn't need them to know his or her worth

You can tell yourself that but it's all in the numbers

The Privilege

Beware the slow snare of Time

As it saps away your strength

You're the unwitting pawn in its lonely losing game

Yet I remember walks down leafy

Lanes in Norwalk, with you and your wise canine companion

And I remember laughter over movies in your upstairs guest room

While we downed those tortilla chips and salty tomato salsa

Or how when I lived there below you

How you sat on my bed and shared experiences

Or the beautiful sea stones you would wear

And how your dining room hosted Angelic messengers

Who surveyed each dinner scene and made me feel safe

As I hold your hand

Which still grips so tight

I know this seems a desperate end

To a beautiful survivor such as you

I still can thank you for the gift of being close to you

You saved me more than I can say

But I have to let go that wish today

While you make a final bow and share this one last day

With me

It has always been a privilege

Don't Get Attached

Don't get attached to the jester in the court

Only Fools pay for Fools to suffer a gladder End

His smile, a dragon in the cave

Is a representation of a caustic Wit

That bit

Not the pretty dreams of lovelorn maidens

Disappearing in and out of the vapors

His hat always in his hand

A ready Imposter

Ready for everything and nothing

All at once

He Snuck Up on Me

Shared history does not a torrid coupling make

A careless comic reference

Or a reference to such skill

As is had by a Rake on the clock

Especially furtive are the glances

They're only mine

An unequivocal defense

A sense of disquietude

While I should down the referendum

My angry Guide insists is valid

A despicable notion

I've lost the will to motion

Have I right or talent to judge?

But those long-loved blue eyes

Are walking away

And I won't stay

Because the player in me has lost the game

Strictly Business

Strictly a matter of business
This waste of my hard-earned time and treasure
They want it all and give nothing in return and
The empty weight of zero coins fills my hands
That shake from the winter ice
And I drove so far again
The offer made, it's always the one I'm with
Who makes the profit -while I sit -
Waiting for interest to unveil the lucky one
Who accepts the gift of me

The Nowhere Plan

We walked this path to nowhere you and I

Childhood friends with shared New England Memory

The kind that never forgives or forgets

I met you when my glasses were bigger than my face

And opened my heart to your white hands

White smoke of contrails erased our moments

And another life in another state swallowed me whole

Trick of the fates thrust you towards me

When I was old enough to vote for lies

And hours were spent in careful contemplation of

Your latest friend-ship sinking

It was always a demon possessing some person

You held dearer to you, whose biting words

Left scars and chew holes in your flesh

And I listened, supporting your story

Coiling your tail so you could strike back at your tale-of-woe

Each time it drew nearer to the time for your knives

Each time I dreamed of you turning on me

And cutting paper devils out to dress in my favorite sweaters

One day the meter ran out on us

And you stood with a mouthful of metal

Nails that you spit 'til at last they drew blood

And so forcefully they shattered even healthy teeth

I waited until those cuts had begun to heal, then tore out the stitches with my fingers

Begging you to return

The strings of skin were still livid and red as I forced open the wound

To heal it

Over time you slipped in salt or lemon, waiting

Until I was breathless on my knees

I looked in the dust-caked mirror thought I saw you there

Instead of my reflection

I took it as a sign

I couldn't flee, was hopeful for a hopeless reunion

The Nowhere Plan in full effect

I'm Not that Stupid

Open my knapsack and give her my apple, They say

Open wide now, let in the viper

How many trucks can hit you at once!

Street-pizza plaything am I –

Take my heart and break it again

And the snow globe with our frosty memories

Fire ants give better company

Though they might leave me starving

They shape the apple in a writhing mass

Rendering it inedible

And indelible reminder of a Toxic You

Knockabout

You're a half-lit candle in the priming dark

The vodka-haze still blinds your eyes

You told me your marriage is a bag of stale bread

And I'm the spicy tequila

Lemon-flavored tears swirl in my tea

I told you the world moves in knockabout waves

Your ship *doesn't* have to come in

The Reflection in the Mirror

As long as I can still see her things are ok

Not narcissistic pleasure but the tether

To my faltering mortality

She Equals Me

A being that, while she's still here

Is slowly fading with every cell death and time-ticking smile

She can move her mouth

And blink her eyes

And stain the sink with toothpaste

And her voice bounces off the blue tiles

Breaking into pieces that make musical breaths

Firewood

I carry the pain that came when you left us

Like firewood – heavy, splintery

Ultimately necessary

To forget you would eat my humanity

And like the fire that leaps from the wood

You burn always

Gold

Gold was all I saw when I looked at you

Gold skin

Gold hair

Even your eyes danced gold-flecked sambas

Never quite an It-Boy

You were clearly so much more

More than the masses could swallow

Though you entertained

It was the gold in you that remained

That lingered in shimmering flakes on their walkways

That gold glints off angel wings now

In the tears of the child you left behind

Things I Want to Tell You

You checked out three Octobers past

Past your inspiration-date

Alice I wish to say

Look at where I've come to now

On my own two feet

I'm not that rapid-breathing mare

Chasing invisible flies

I'm real now

Functional

Powerful

Taken in the right context

I share this Leap with you

Secret Friend

Blueberry Muffins

I never liked blueberries

Most times they were met with crinkled nose and gagging tongue

Until one day –

A grey and impersonal day –

With leaves lying on dry ground

Anemic in their uselessness

The day my mortality introduced itself to me

The little dreamer with the big-eyed stare

Who at thirty-four still found pleasure in the golden crayon

And the Barbie curls – even Lego blocks

Who sucked her brittle thumb as she curled away

From the broken world

I missed the little moments that form the basis of an average day

And I hadn't even left yet!

I opened my hungry mouth

And inhaled, perhaps for the first time

The cinnamon crumble of blueberry muffins

On Hurricane Sandy

I was born on an island, then whisked away

I remember her green trees

Framing the yard where I chased monarch

Butterflies I could stubbornly swear were Viceroys

And I remember a sunburned seashore

And Christopher's Spiderman shirt

I see my island now – broken ship-hull skeletons

And houses that vomited their intestines in an Ebola-parody

Pretty shells no longer where they belong

Desperately searching the eroded beach

The place I lived, the place I loved

They lie in cruel wet ruin

My island, my Sea

Can it be enemy to me?

How can a sea calm me now?

When it is fierce and ravenously hungry

Destined to flatten and submerge?

Twinkling in the sun, jewel among jewels

She's a lurking Hydra

Who flings rocks and brackish water in her tantrum

As King Neptune nods gravely at us all

Society Says

Society says I'm thirty-five

So I should be knee-deep in Blue's Clues

And sticky sippy cups

And I should spell out the naughty words

Society says I'm a eunuch

Because I still think sex is sacred –

A dance to share with a holy partner

And not some nit-wit you met at a bar named Slappy's

Society says, society says

Ah to hell with what Society says!

<u>Not that Kind of Girl</u>

He sees a hopeful sign in his world

Tiny green-eyed atom in a multi-verse of Slut

She's not what you dreamed a 32-C blonde would be

The shop's been closed since '78

But the door's been left unlocked

Around her it's not 20 inches of snow

Or a howling blizzard

She's the fire licking at the walls

Not that frigid Queen of Ice you say

Not a prostitute or a Sandra Fluke

He pauses, wondering where his angel went

Secretly glad she is gone

No longer poised at the door of the gentlemen's club

Thinks more of leaving his dollars in the collection plate at Church

I Hope He Knows (for an ALS Patient)

I hope he knows he's not a statue

That's he's still so much a man

Though the circuitry's worn out

And the gentle voice is gone

I hope he's not dreaming at night

Of running

Of Passes

Of cuddling his wife and son

For that would be too cruel

But the universe has tricked our Hero

Left him to be operated like a fleshly mannequin

Poseable arms

And daily changings

But a soul fights on through the mechanics of a voice box

The man still stands as tall

Though he cannot stand at all

Hat Infection

Oh she who is the wearer of many hats

Steward of the Great Divide

A course in Cause and Effect

A malevolent wish for anonymity

She's hooked to the silver blood of the laptop

Or coasting down a river of doubt about

Her forsaken quest for Ability

Hoping for a taste of sterility

In a corner of the salivating world which doesn't judge or push her too hard

Mice run in confused circles at her feet

With music that penetrates like acid

Swirling through their tiny brains

They paint the metaphor that is her own mind

A seething storm of magnificent strength

The hats have all become too tight

Like they're stapled to her head by unruly children

With an appetite for the Absurd

The Emperor and the Energy Healer

The Emperor stood, so vast and wise

His scepter snarled in the beam of moon

He summoned the Lady with elven tongue

Bathing his regrets in moonlit sherry

She lay her ghostlike hands

On temples that housed his sometimes beneficent mind

The loving light that seeped through her

Caressed his tense features

And smoothed the jagged cliffs of his face

One night the Emperor called in his sleep

For the maiden's healing touch

His heart grew as the sleep of the sated conquest took him

The last time his angel sat at his feet

Her palm on his chest

Bright brown eyes that had overseen a thousand executions

Forgiveness left a trail of salt

And she wiped it away with a corner of her meager dressing gown

He presented the ring that had graced

The hand of many Queens before

But the healer bowed her head

Softly blew away like dandelion spores

To bloom in another Emperor's garden

The Castle and the Core Crew

I climbed these stairs in a time that was weighted down

With the howls of mail-clad youth as they

Trembled into manhood

I remembered them well

These soldiers I trained to

Conquer and cast aside their mentor

Their thundering steeds and weapons that drew their shine from the sun

As they pounded on, lasting more than a fortnight

In their Vision and Endurance, crafting the Master Plan

I knew them more deeply than they knew themselves

And in my heart blasted their blood

A metaphor swiftly taking the place of Truth and accurate Report

Oh the Rapport we had!

In a past life we rode together, these horsemen and commander

Drinking the sour ale that bled through our sweat

And our makeshift camaraderie

Our ghosts imprint on the stone in these walls

And I fondly, creakily, and somewhat sneakily

Remember the Castle and the Core Crew

The Hard-Luck Coin

She cries in the midst of a dandy day

Sheltered from brimstone and wet from the bay

She's hurried and worried and wrecked by her dread

And crumbles the flowers that lie long dead

Her hands migrate towards a tower of money

Then wipe at eyes that are bloody-red-runny

She picks mournfully at a salty white page

Hiding from the need to engage

With the ratter that's sliming against her cold walls

Whose heart is filled with nothing at all

She's moaning and praying and trying to pretend her quilted world isn't fraying

The Ones at the door are pounding it down

Stomping and cursing and the crime they have found

When they break down her door she knows what's in store

She's played this bruising game before

The hard-luck coin came to town once more

He Cried to the Phantom

He cried to the phantom in the dusky eve
Molten river coursing down through the crags of his face
His heart hearing only the breaking of a wand
His magic a disheartened spark that poofed away
His black eyes looked blue from the vantage point the devils had
Blue with the water of steamy tears
Blue with the iciness that fills a numbed interior
The floating menace streamed across the damp leaves
Shuddering and shuttering and crazily muttering
Wherefore art thou black prince of pain and purpose?
Shaky hands faded in faded out
'Til at last sleep overtook the war-fed lout
He held the last letter she wrote
Hoping the Phantom could still read the words

Bacteria God (An Atheist's Lament)

You tell me we're Bacteria

That no magic lies within our blankety-blank world

That we don't transcend the biological

At our fabulously inconsistent core

I'm confused and confounded

By Religion and its Whore

A community of cultists who follow blindly and trust the words of the Virus

I'm lost you're lost

Lost on the merry-go-round of a childhood dream

Forever tainted

Heavy

You only want to lift things up

When they aren't heavy

It takes so much work to work you and me

Even if we agreed to proceed cautiously

It's doubly hard to get through the day

When I can't figure out the safe thing to say

Inside is a heart you tell me is live

And full of a gentle love with no lies

The kind, that into a storybook melts

But who can ignore the emotional welts!

Of a 2012 man with iPhones for hands

Who tosses a word, doesn't care how it lands

And one who chiefly ignores a desire

Whose five-o'clock shadow leaves hidden the fire

I'm dumb and I'm lazy and stubborn with him

According to the playbook, he's right and he wins -

You only want to lift things up

When they aren't heavy

Why Do I Come When They Pray?

Lord there's a question, been dying to ask

Never made sense, I'm not up to your task!

Sometimes they expect so much from this tired old sinner

Sometimes I want so much to quell all their fears

Why do I come when they pray?

Is my heart a hotline to some Ascended Master?

How can I serve them when I can't even cook

Up the recipe for happiness for me?

The broken they swarm and I hold out both hands to catch them

Falling somehow

Calling my name in their choking whispers

Why do I come when they pray?

I arrive it seems, on breath of God

Driven by the ceaseless wind of wing-beats

I hold them yet it's never enough

I listen with kindness for days they want months

They tell me they don't believe in God or Heaven

Yet their begging seems to pull me

They pull harder, I drag forward,

Coping with their mysteries, badly

Bluntly forcing my song's consuming power

Over their new and aimless silence

Why do I come when they pray?

The little helper

The Laoe Paradox

Devil mated with Angel - The Orgiastic Monastic

Seraphim surefire spawned from the Chaos

Of brightness in the skies

Why I come when they pray?

I wait for the answer that never comes

And believe the warrior-throne will empty for an empty Me

And kiss away the tears of stupefied sheep

Pocket Blonde

Pocket blonde

With a control-box that's out of control

Quick! Hit the button!

No not that one!

And no – that wire is so frayed

It makes her afraid

She moves her doll eyes to the sky

Her hands clench that frustrated clench

Overwrought broken toy

She needs winding

She stumbles with that Ativan-gait

She's over seasoned

But a lack of reason clouds her judging smile

She's a tiny prize

In the candlelight she moves like a specter with a Plan

Malfunctioning

Maladjusted

And needs to have her attitude adjusted
Put her away

Back in her box to keep her safe

And leave plenty of room for tissues

Just Kidding

Just kidding

It's like the puppeteer is jerking the strings

Then tying them round my neck

Hoping to see me suspended – Lo! The Arc!

Swollen – here's the red carpet

Here's the solution

Then Oh! The squeeze!

Ultimo-squeeze!

Does it need to be a walking abortion?

Non-viable and existing in borrowed time

When does Santa Claus stop pulling back the bag of goodies?

I'm gritting down

Bearing down

Baring myself, the responsible whore – wait –

Just kidding

Promises made, promises that erupt from undisciplined mouths

It's bad and it's bleak

And the perps squeak away

Getting away during a clean streak

Making a clean sweep

Of the premises where I still held hope

That my work could be justified

But I'm blinded by stupidity

The frigid waters sucking me down

To drown

Just kidding

I can't grant wishes they say, enjoy the red tape!

I see it shred

Hope dances like a firefly in summer's jowls

And this tiny thing howls

As they shake their heads

Pet me with condescension and say

Just kidding

Things that Can Only Be Broken

My heart – like a fountain

Pours out its love

To the muse with the musical tattoo

I hurt in impressive amounts

Don't you see

The fairness of an unfair trade

A beauty forlorn, gazing in her crystal ball

Talking to walls that can only talk back

To other walls

She holds these feelings close to her

Gently rocking them and their baby vampire teeth

Loving the things that can only be broken

The Box Where It Lives

The box where it lives

A pain so alien and yet so alarmingly deep in its flowing

Almost carnal - its knowing -

I put it in the space between worlds

Where the specters of my dead loved ones roam

I light the candle - in memoriam -

The timing is true

The aim fair slight

A sleight-of-hand trick you played with the broken soul who loves you

The box where it lives

Agony and desire - fighting for

Each other's hand in marriage

As, to be no more?

On this sunny frigid day

I heal

Incand-Ecstasy

We're bright, you and I

But are we supernovas

Exploding out of a fiery space

Are we too hot to ever properly touch?

And are the mountains

That ring this sleepyville-land

Silent monuments to a light that bespoke Divinity?

Besotted are they with our

Electric light-wave masquerade

As we flitter and flutter

Fizzle and sputter

Sparking like broken wires

And coming alight in the most beautiful way

The Wasp in the Jar

I'm shaking so shake me up

There's no way out and there's no way up

Can't catapult to catch some sky

They told me so long ago

I had escapist dreams

And an imagination to capture triumph

But the mountains closed in

And crushed my worker-bee hands beneath them

I thought that Once could come Again

That rocks wouldn't hold my backpack down

Buzzing and maddened by the play-by-play

They're watching me lose my foothold

They're laughing

.